Trouble Light

Trouble Light

Poems
by

Gerald McCarthy

West End Press

Thanks to the following publications in which some of these poems first appeared: *Broome Review, Italian Americana, New Letters and New Letters Reader II, Nimrod, The Pedestal, Poet Lore, Rattle, Riverwind, Silk Road, TriQuarterly,* and *War, Literature & The Arts*.

Different versions of some poems in this collection were first published in the following magazines and anthologies: *America, The And Review, Café Review, Encounter, Enskyment, Mid-American Review, A New Geography of Poets, Post Traumatic Press, Primo, Rattle,* and *White Pelican Review*.

"Spanish Steps" appeared in *Wild Dreams: The Best of Italian Americana,* Fordham University Press, 2008.

"Among ghosts" was featured as "Ghosts" on the compact disc *Biting the Tongue,* performed by Frank Messina and Spoken Motion.

The author wishes to thank the American Academy in Rome for two visiting artist residencies that provided time and space to complete some of the poems in this collection, and the Cumberlidge Foundation for summer and fall residencies in the Umbrian countryside.

Special thanks to Michael Henson for his kind and thoughtful advice concerning the final editing and revision of the manuscript.

First edition, November 2008
Paperback: ISBN 978-0-9816693-0-4
Price: $12.95

Cover painting: Gas Station Playground by Ralph Fasanella. Courtesy of ACA Galleries, New York City.
Photograph of Gerald McCarthy by Dennis Galante.
Cover design by Nancy Woodard.
Text design by Gian Lombardo

West End Press, P.O. Box 27334, Albuquerque, NM 87125
www.westendpress.org

Contents

Four

for Michele

—*Every stone has its story,*
Every wind speaks its mind, and there is
A birth giving, a bringing-forth of days
That is not time, but space; memory;
The irrecoverable home.

Paul Zweig

One

Teasel

If you hold anything long enough
there's bound to be trouble.
It will break apart
a little cup of light,
a sound of rain in open fields.

If you find this spiny flower
pick it up, remember
another fall, a time when the cold
came too quickly and caught the weeds too—
the frost rising into mist,
the mist disappearing.

Today catnip and henbit,
wood sorrel, chicory and brooms edge,
and still you keep looking for its crown
of thorns,
a blue dash in fallen leaves
above the culvert edge.

You know the railroad bed leads
to the creek, and the creek opens
out into the river, and the river
moves southward toward the sea.

At night, you listen for the trooper cars—
the sirens circle the neighborhood,
a convict in the marsh.
You think he must have got away
that prisoner,
the man they chased
through river nettles
as the season turned cold.
The morning paper

ran a photograph of the river,
night-lights and search boats.

Today, walking above stone paths
near the water's edge,
you see the pale blue streak in the brown woods
and you know it's there.

Pylon

And the young ones?
In the coffins.
   —Miguel Hernandez

At night,
aluminum boxes
slide down steel rollers
out of the belly of a plane.

Names from a new wall
count off a kind of cadence,
marking time
no one hears.

Trucks wait to upload
their cargo.
Shadows edge the airstrip,
a greasy rain begins to fall.

On a line by Li Po

Second snow of November,
already the high peaks are white
in the blue distance.

I think of my first
homecoming,
I see myself bent double
carrying duffels down from a train—
city lights,
the war far away.

A great horned owl's cry
pierces the dark,
and I think
of *what ruins our lives.*

Winter Solstice 2005 (the new war dead)

A flock of starlings
scuttle on the rooftop
splash in rainwater pools.
The last leaves hang in the branches
of the red maple tree.
Look, my friend says
there's a kind of dark
all around us,
you have to get used to it.
Bricker's neighbor shot himself in his garage
the summer I turned eleven.
A *pistol,* Tommy said, *Smith & Wesson* .38.
Once in winter I cut the yards,
saw him bent over his workbench—
the trouble light overhead,
cigarette smoke.
He saw my shadow and looked up.
He drove an old gray Plymouth,
a car with a single headlight like a beak.
Birdman of Church Street, we called him.
Now December rain keeps falling
and the news slips out.
The dead come back.
A line of graying birds
huddle together in the rain.

Gathering firewood at Chimney Mountain

Snow falling
in the mountain stillness,
a humpbacked shadow
startles me
against the stand of bare trees.
Could I have come this far
already?
Too soon, too soon—
memory *like a fire*
we keep lighting
that keeps going out.

The wounded

There's a kind of slanting late winter light
out on the edge of a field,
so when you look closely it's like a border,
only fluid, moving.
A group of wild turkeys
feeds on the juniper and bearberries
near the entrance to what the locals call
the other Arlington—
a hillside cemetery off the old King's Highway,
and that light is coming toward them.
If you listen you can hear
the soft clucking sounds they make.
Today in the glare of the supermarket light,
my son makes me look at lobsters
piled on one another in a plastic tank.
They don't move much in there, he says.
They're stunned, I tell him,
their claws taped up, waiting.
Outside in the late March dusk
a cold rain on stone, you think of them—
trapped in their tanks
or hospital beds.

For a friend in prison

Today the newspaper headlines—
NEW DEATH PENALTY BILL APPROVED.
A letter on the table—
an extended sentence
upstate. I see your face
behind the pages.
I hear the gate guard
cough and shake his keys
loose.
A voice says: One, coming in.
The electric door slides shut.
After shackling your hands and ankles,
the guards lead you down a tunnel
toward the D Block cell.

Don't look back
for Raymond Patterson

I see him poised, stoop-shouldered,
too tall for the lectern,
reading the poem about his uncle—
who kept a rock in his pocket
to remind him of what home was really like.

At Douglass' grave in Mt. Hope Cemetery
we saw the stones lined up,
stones others had placed there,
each one a different shape
and weight.

Our homes have changed
and changed again,
but our past
we carry with us like a weight,
a stone we can't let go.

Maybe for me
it's a group of soldiers singing
in tidewater swamp,
what love has joined together—
the Carolina dusk rising around us.
And in that there is a part of your life,
what you have left when it's late
and Ben Webster plays
a single petal of a rose.

Outside the fall has almost gone—
a reflection in the glass, dusk
and the voice, not your own
taken from you
like a stone rubbed smooth by the years,

passed from hand to hand
until someone says—*he's gone,
you know.*

Ars poetica

The note from the editor says—
send new poems
when you have the chance
and do mention that these
were a near miss—
they made it to the final round.

Oh yes, like driving all night from Lakeville
to Kiss My Ass, and stopping often
to throw another quart of oil in,
you know, smoke billowing out—
like that time you picked up a hitchhiker
near the Indiana line,
a tower painter who'd worked
all fall painting steel towers with mitts,
a hundred feet up, he said
and two buckets strapped to me.
All night you drove him west, until you hit the snow
in Iowa.

You can't drive all night into snow country
west of Dubuque
without thinking of the things
you learned from the road—
how to feather the gas
to keep the carburetor from icing up,
how to ease into the long straight-aways
and keep your eyes focused.

You paid for your mistakes,
waiting in semicircle
the sting of a calloused palm against your neck,
reciting the words carefully
—*a slow steady pressure to the rear*

until the sear is engaged, the trigger
released.

After you've been hit enough
you stop blinking,
the road leads out
of the labyrinth of days
you called your childhood,
out of the near miss
and frightened screech of tires.

Two

Susquehanna

Morning, a rose-colored blush
against the windshield.
The names of small towns
drift past.
The route sign fades,
a white hand waving
twelve more miles.

Now I know the way.
The years scatter
like a shower of sparks
in the rear-view mirror.

*

Shadow, the greenskeep,
leans out over his mower
and calls my name.
I lift the steel pin,
push open the wire gate.
The tractor jerks ahead,
a clumsy moth shredding sunlight
into its canvas wings.

I watch it cross the morning fairways.
He showed me
the river nettles that caused a rash,
choke weed, knotweed
and toothwort.

*

The humpback Dodge is a blur
in the glass storefronts.
My father turns the wheel
to the right, hands straining
against his anger.

He leads me back to the field, lets me fight
each of the boys in turn.
As long as it's fair,
he yells,
and pushes me forward.

I hold on to the rail and he goes down again.
I can see his eyes open, his hand
grabs my hair, pulling me under.

*

The mist clings like smoke,
a haze along the river's edge.
I remember campfires in August,
night fishing near the pumping house.
I cross the steel bridge above the creek,
the golf course stretches out
like a green dream
of summer.

Blue road, blue shadows. . .
on the river, the carp
begin to feed
in the first rush of sunlight.

Note in a bottle

The Erie-Lackawanna trains are the ghosts
of summer nights.
A town of freight yards,
tanning factories, time clocks.
A town that smelled like leather.

I walk the ties through yards
and loading docks, remember
crawling between rails,
watching the headlights of sheriff cars.
If I listen I can almost hear the sirens,
glimpse the smudge of orange sky
beyond the smokestacks.

I push open the door to Ernie's Grill
on the North Side of town, the Italian side.
His hands stained brown from shoe dye,
John Robinsky cursed the heat, swore
the union would never get in.

It never did.
They quit making leather from cowhide.
They closed the factories,
laid off the workers.

Robinsky raised pigeons because it was
something he could do.
We used to watch them lift off
and carry those messages away.
Nobody answered, John.
No one heard anything
but that flapping of wings.

The gun lifted, the glass raised.
Soot-filled years in the attic
with the wire cages.
Mornings in the steel vats, the drying sheds.
Nobody counted.
A town of mortgages, parking lots.

I walk home toward my father's house,
toward a light in the window of an upstairs room
that flickers and goes out.

Frankie

Illusions are the only true
substantial things
  —Leopardi

There's a song, but you can't sing it,
it's not yours anymore.
And if you look up it's October,
you rise from the basement
concrete dust in your hair,
kneepads puff your pant legs out.
There's nowhere to go.
You smoke a cigarette
watch the cars slowing for the curve
in the lake road.
You hear the sound of waves on the breakwall.
They've sent you back
to redo the job the main crew lost—
recap it with an inch of new mud
and *make it smooth,*
the crew boss says.
You can't reason with it,
the afternoon's almost gone.
Dusk will find you
at a ridge roadhouse,
its steamy windowpanes
a blur of towns with names
like Pike and Trout and Nunda.
There's a day,
but you can't get it back.

The arc welder

At Kellog's Welding in York, New York
John Kellog lifts his hand
and the thin seam of light
moves with him, the glow
scatters in a shower of sparks
on the wooden floor.
And with one motion
he makes the harrow whole again.

The tractor moves, the earth pushes up.
He turns his back to the fields,
to the farmer hunched over the gears,
plowing the furrows in the dusk.
There is only the darkened shop,
the light feeding in through the open door,
and his daughter's voice outside
rising in play.

His back to the light,
hands grip the iron bar,
he says: *I know*
she wants me home, but this wheel
won't wait, and grinning
he flips the spark guard down,
he lights the torch.

Island Lake

The dirt road ends in blackberry thicket
an outcrop of stone—*highrock*
the Cayuga called it.

Through the evergreen, the silver maple,
the birch, six lakes like drops of blue mist,
each one a mirror.

*

We stared at the planes
through the stereo viewer
until we were blind with silver,
my brother straddling
the rail, his face
pushed up against my own.
A wall to the roar of engines,
a small hole in the future.
And how many more years to know
the thrust, the liftoff?

There is a platform
crowded with faces, a window
opening like the shutter of a camera.
And the fields become one glimpse
among many.

*

My uncle cracks his knuckles
and stares at his hands—*piecework*,
he says, shaking his head.

Laid-off from Fisher Body in Flint,
he's come east to package shoes.

His days off he'd climb out of the valley
hunting for mushrooms in the hedgerows.
He showed me how to cross the open places,
to ease down the creek bank to find the ones
that were good to eat.
Later, we washed them in the well sink,
the white caps bobbing in the tub,
his hands pushing their tiny heads under.

*

TJ smiles and says the Legion boys
are buying.
All through the afternoon we worked,
setting the forms for the feed mill.
At night we'd drink in the small-town bars,
shooting eight ball until it was too late
to do anything but sleep.
The five a.m. wake-ups, the foreman yelling:
let's go, let's pour it out.
A dream of Friday nights, of dollars
slid across copper-topped counters.

*

Far below a boat casts off,
its ripples widening.
My grandfather leans forward,
his forehead wrinkles,
his thick fingers slip the hook
into the water beetle
as he lets the line spin out—

blue nylon circles arc
above the water.
And drawing close
he whispers: *watch,*
watch how they rise to it.

*

My brother calls from the backyard—
the shadows of a church, of a time
I said I was sorry and meant it.
He calls, but now I cannot hear him,
and we are running side by side
as if to outrun memory itself.
As if we could outdistance
the smokestacks, the vacant lots
the VA homes,
and in some hollow on the cliffs,
share the afternoon,
the blur of traffic
from the world below
calling us both away.

Ghazal of Our Lady of Good Counsel

Here's the pew where we waited for confession
here the wood worn smooth by our hands.

Yes, here is the dark booth where the priest sat,
the soft click of the screen opening.

Here too a smell of incense—
a voice asking how many times?

Then the sigh of his voice giving penance—
prayers for the sin, for forgiveness.

This the aisle where we waited, leaning on stone walls,
the colors of the stained glass windows—stations of the cross.

These are the doors we opened—leading outward.
This is the light that found us in early evening.

Dusk, dusk. Even the birdsongs were still
as the light gave way. These are the stone steps.

Remember? This is the way back.
Listen for the voices murmuring in prayer.

Listen for the chant, for the intonation.
Here, stand beside me again, hush, hush.

Listen for the soft click of the rosary beads,
the smooth rustle of cassocks.

Go on out and walk home through the smoke
the piles of leaves burning along the roadside.

A beggar on horseback

One morning I caught Red Stanko
pulling empties from recycle bins
stacked along the side of our house.
Red smiled, said
for smokes.
He carried his tote of empties
like a sack of rabbits,
crossed into the neighbor's yard.

Now his son's got the junker
Red used to drive,
he howls down the street, and I think
old Red is still alive—
until I see Mike driving
and I know.

They say cancer got him fast.
I thought jail, or worse
when I didn't see him,
but no the neighbor said
he's dead.
And now his wife and son
are back at grandma's house again.
My father used to say
put a beggar on horseback
and he'll break his neck—
but Red, he never got the chance to ride,
unless it was some old rig
he'd fixed and drove until it let him down.
I see him still
playing football with the boys in the street—
toothless, grinning,
he calls the signals.

Floorwalker

In this photograph circa 1956,
the dead woman in the casket
laid out in the dining room of her own home
is someone I do not know,
someone who worked for my stepmother
at the shoe factory downtown,
a floorwalker.
I listen to the other women cry,
or talk in whispers
as if the dead woman could hear.
My stepmother makes me sit near the window
and I can see the woman
stretched out in front of me—violets,
dampness, her eyes closed.

Years later I learned a floorwalker
was someone who checked the other workers
on each floor of the factory.
She walked all day.

At the field north of Scranton
my uncle showed me
how to raise the shotgun,
he laughed when the others said—
it'll knock him down.

And that's just what it did,
my shoulder sore for a week.
Everything has a kick to it,
he said on our way home,
sitting across from me in the dark.

Mary

She laughs at the screen, the figures
float away in the blue haze.
At lunch she talks of the coalmines,
and my grandfather moves through the half-light.
But now it is a cave she comes to,
a tunnel of black smoke,
and her voice rises, trills.
She is a girl of six,
afraid of the night sky closing,
surrounding the terraced hills.
She answers across the miles
of connections, but does not know me.
She works on black leather uppers in the factory,
walks home with her sisters through knee-high drifts.
Now there are other rooms she does not know.
She folds white towels end to end,
presses them smooth on a steel table.
Tonight she will not eat or sleep.
She paces the floor, climbs the stair,
clicks the light on as she goes,
mumbles something about the moon, the boarders
getting up for work.

Coffee

My father leans against the glass—*it's out there,*
he says, pointing to the river beyond the window,
you can't see it, it's too dark.

Now I drink coffee in a Styrofoam cup,
I hold the cup as if it were fragile,
as if it were fine crystal.

And I hear my father's voice as if he were still here—
he sits in the front seat of his old Dodge
drinking coffee, we're driving that car out of the valley.

We pass the factories, the viaduct
he used to cross on Fridays to get the payroll out.
And he smiles, as if time stood still.

He tells me the story about bailing out of the B-29
into the jungles of Burma. It's 1944,
and my father has just turned thirty five.

They fly *the hump* from China to Burma
to India—and an engine catches fire.
I can see the smoke billow out of the fuselage.

My father stands in the doorway, poised with his parachute.
The co-pilot broke his leg, he says,
and we had to carry him for six days in the monsoon.

It gets dark and I see him clearly again,
hunched in the cone of light at the kitchen table.
He looks up from his columns of figures,

asks what I want, his voice tired and gruff.
He looks down at me over his glasses.
And when I don't answer, he says—*it's time for bed.*

My father used to send notes to my brother and me,
lists of the money he'd sent us over the years.
There were columns of figures:

Fifty dollars—birthday gift, seventy-five—Christmas.
When I moved him, I found his notebook, a twin column
stenographer pad, our names on opposing pages.

After he started to forget things, he insisted
he had a payroll to put out, that they'd hired him back
at eighty-five—to keep the records straight.

I found those record books too, and in a back drawer
an old newspaper clipping—
my father kneeling with the flight crew after their rescue.

Now, I listen as he calls out those names—Hopbottom,
Chittenango, Nanticoke. We drive the foothills,
drink coffee, talk about what might have been.

Migrant labor camp #7

No one knows
where the day goes,
but someone is counting
bushels of cabbages
stacked in wooden crates.
They pile up like the pale
heads of another dead,
on their way to cities,
canning factories,
shopping carts.
No news is good news,
he says, shaking his head.
The gas heat swells
the cubicle, yellowing
everything in a false dawn.
And I see his eyes
as he passes me the bottle,
pushes me —
no, but I heard Lady sing once, he says.

Station to station

In Johnson City at Tri-City Beverage
in 1968, Sully and I
pulled quart bottles of ginger ale
two at a time from conveyor belts.

We stacked the wooden cases row on row,
the pallets pushed against spinning metal rollers.
The first day a bottle slipped
exploding on the concrete floor,
I shook, startled at the sound.
The crew boss laughed and shook his head,
you never know, he said.

Down the line
the dispatcher called out—
two-five, four-five.
The bottles
clinked, slid toward us in wet rows.

We ate our lunch out in the open
straddling the stacks of empty pallets
in the company yard.

You don't have to be a genius, Sully said,
to see where this job leads.
Broke, spending our last dollars
in a factory bar, I knew
I had to leave some things behind—the town,
the long days of work,
and Sully, gone half-crazy with his own years
there, alone, grinning in the half-light.

We inherit grief, it clings like sweat,
like the ribbon of blood

from a wound
that will not heal.
Above the main street, the arches widened
like the road, etched with the words—
Home of the Square Deal,
erected by the workers.

Three

A gift

The day my mother died
my father gave me
a metal space pistol—
it would whir and spark
when I pulled the trigger back.
I was four years old then
and did not understand,
but I saw my father's tears
how his hands shook
when he gave me the toy,
and I knew
I would not see her again.

Years later,
aiming a rifle at a figure
who ran along a hillside,
I thought of my father—
the afternoon we walked together
through the neighborhood,
the words rising around us
until I could not see.
And as I squinted at the man
a dark speck
moving through the elephant grass,
I did not squeeze the trigger
I jerked it back
so the round hit the tree line,
the man out of range
safe, but still running.

*

Now again
my father sits across from me,
yet it is my mother
I see—
curled into the folds
of a hospital bed.
Today my son
comes downstairs for breakfast;
he laughs, pushes
a pencil into my father's hand,
asks him to draw
a boat with sails—
a magic one that spins
and whirls.
I watch the two of them
together, Nick
slides on his chair,
his head bent as my father sketches
the outline of the prow—
how long it's taken us
to try to forgive each other.

Hook Mountain Lookout
to Aeneas in the lower world

Like you we learned to find our way
past harbors lashed with winter,
our ships deserted
run aground, left to break up in the waves.

Oh name, we asked, give us a name,
but the roads led away—
the timetables yellowing
like the smoky light of dawn in southern stations,
choked with the tainted sulfur air
of paper mills and scrap yards.

We might have turned back and asked
for time, but it was late,
time was not ours.
That day in prison, Beacon said:
Time is a wall, color
will not change it.

We watched the shadows
fill the morning yards,
the snowdrifts like froth against stone piers.
I think of the others now—
Big Mike in Tampa
staring past the smoke of an after-hours club,
drunk with the light of new dawn.
He held the troopers off for hours,
gave in to the straitjacket
the glare of headlines.

Or Sonny facing his square of daylight,
sweet Sonny who followed the tracks home,
home ringing in his ears

like a street of dreams
and dream salesmen.

Time you are cold, Beacon said.
And the snow kept falling,
filling in the crevices of stone walls.

Here the dusk comes glittering
brackish, wafting above the inland sea,
as if regret came in the fading light
silencing even these stone hallways.

for W.D. Ehrhart

Against the rain
for Sharif, Jimmy Z., Fitz and Sonny

This morning
a meadowlark in the poplars
against the rain that rises
and disappears.
I remember asking:
where will I go? how far is it?

Today is the Fourth of July,
the flags are hung from porches,
the bells ring out their own cadence.
Ray Chunn grabs my arm in the prison hallway
after his two months in *the box.*

This memory is of smoke, of the yard
littered with a world turned over,
a stain that keeps spreading into all the pictures.

I drive home, listen to the weather report
the weekend traffic toll.
The noise of fireworks catches me off guard.

Among ghosts

I don't know where it is
you have gone,
what street, what prison cell
what solitary room you call
your own,
or if you lie in a city graveyard
and restless, haunt the alleyways,
the late night eateries.

Each autumn I think I see you
when the last of the maple leaves
begin to fall.

I see you poised
like some graceful crane
against a parking meter—
your dungaree leg pinned up,
your back to the traffic,
the drivers' stares.

Yet, each time
as I reach out to touch
your shoulder,
it's some other man who turns
grinning, hawklike,
and extends his hand,
offering a bunch of paper flowers
each one like a tiny flame
twisted from a string of flames.

Roads

I too have known roads
white, rutted dirt roads
where the stones popped
tore at the underside of the car.
Sunflower roads,
roadsides littered with wild chicory and broom.
Steep, stony roads
where the rain washed the gravel down
so the car slid and dipped in the wash of sand.
I have not forgotten you—white rose
plucked from the mouth of summer.
You, odor of jasmine, gardenia,
rising amidst the sweat and thrust of movement.
Roads that led me away from you
from the summer day you fell to me,
your arms full of flowers—
sweet breath of the new-mown fields.
How many roads it took
for us to reach each other.

Ora e sempre

Maybe the best graves stay unmarked,
the right words never find themselves cut into stone
—Richard Hugo

If it were up to me
I'd scatter these ashes near
the places you loved—*Spuyten duyvil*
the East River, the dark rocky banks
where you swam as a boy.
I'd hold a service at St. Stephen's Church
in Manhattan, its frescoes painted
by an out-of-work Brumidi,
later maybe we'd visit Woodlawn
where my grandmother lies
and my first born son next to her.

If it were up to me,
I'd do anything to keep you
from going back upstate
to the town where everyone died,
where even the living know a cold
and loneliness I can't answer,
where the streets have turned back,
the maples gone, the fields gone.
I can't change what's done—
the things I didn't say or said too late.
They say music makes us whole again,
but this song's in pieces.

for my father

44 ∼

Jumper
Variations on a line by Guido Gozzano

Maybe the world is a place
of fear and isolation,
and those who stand
on the lip of things
go mad.
You can't stop it,
you can't bring her back
from that edge.
It's too high, too far.
It's happened
yet *no one knows how*
it happened.
We are left alone with our day
and time is short—
but Auden's lines
are about Spain
and not
a late November day
of freezing rain—
when a fine snow
began ticking the windows
and she stopped the car,
a blue car parked along the rail.
She *went over so fast*
a driver said—
we couldn't stop her.
It happened.
Yet no one knows how.

Daydream

He watches his sons play football in the street,
listens as they yell to one another,
their hands reach for the ball.
And then unexpectedly,
he thinks of the other one,
imagines him there too,
sees him as he never has before—
tall and gangly, too tall for thirteen,
a boy with his mother's quick good looks,
her curly hair, but with my eyes,
my shyness—he says to himself,
half believing his own lie.
And because no one is there, he lets himself
go on with it,
he sees the son's room:
books stacked in odd piles,
banners from Il Palio in Siena,
a horse race they never saw, a stone tower,
toy knights,
falcon kites suspended above the bed.
He sits down there and looks out across the yards.

A small song for Luke

Whenever I see piles of leftover snow
gray and muddied by the new spring,
whenever the first snowcaps
push up from the tufts of frozen earth,
and spring seems to pulse and then
fade, whenever the light lasts
too long—stark and stretched out
like a line of smoke,
I think of you.

Twenty years ago
I drove all night through a Midwest snowstorm
in the old Ford pickup that bucked through the drifts
until I lost control of the wheel—
off the road and
over the edge.
And in those few moments before
the crash, I thought I knew
what pain and loss were, I thought
I knew what it was to drive
all night through a storm that did not end.

I came to against the rail,
the snow pressing in around the windows,
my body tilted sideways in the cab,
and I knew the drifting snow had saved me.

Today, looking down,
caught off guard by soft petals
scattered, spread like clusters of new light,
I called your name, as if
in that harsh one syllable
I might find more than this
hollowed-out place in my side.

Bicycle in the rain

It's true I left your bicycle out in the rain.
I rode it downhill,
cruising the river road,
left it lying on its side
in our friend's yard.
For months it sat there rusting
until it was ruined.
It's been years since I thought of that bike,
but yesterday
as I listened to your voice,
I thought of you
riding that bike
through those city streets,
up in Buffalo.
I've seen college girls ride their bikes
and I imagined you
riding downhill on a sunny fall day.
I saw how lovely you were,
how young and unafraid,
and how fine that three-speed bike was—
its blue gray fenders shiny and new,
and I thought about what you gave up
those small things no one thanks you for
or when they do, it's too late.
I thought of the things you must have wanted
riding to class on your blue bike,
where you hoped to go,
the places you wanted to see.
I thought of the dreams you must have had,
not that I could hope
to know your dreams—but I knew
you had dreams different from the realities
you are left with now.

Mi ricordo

This morning
a flock of seabirds
flew above the waves,
and the light rose above the foam.
Seeing you
in a white blouse
made me remember
a time before our children came,
when you waited for me
quiet and alone.
Hey, I want to say
it's not the waves alone
that let us remember—
time has its way with us
and memory needs a little something
to stir it up.
So much hail,
Vallejo wrote—
that I recall the mouth
of every storm.

Four

Attica 1977

A *skull*
my friend says, *it's like*
you're inside a skull.
And then I feel the pressure
the way the ceilings push down.
I hunch up,
tuck my neck into my shirt.
The deeper I go in
the more the tunnel narrows.
The first time I didn't know
the soft yellow patches
in the wooden beams
filled with plastic wood
were bullet holes.
Yeah, Mustafa said,
you need to look up,
see what's around you.

*

Near Christmas, the class was small
two men were locked down, and the others
off the count—too late to make it,
so only three men showed, Shea
laughed, pulled out
a thin jailhouse joint.
We smoked it there,
watched the snow fall in the yards,
outside.
And then we read
to each other, the words
spinning out.

On my way home
I skidded in the drifts—
first left, then right
until the tires grabbed.
I thought of the floodlights
and the snow-filled yards, tiny barred windows
aglow in the storm.
I thought of the troopers in the rain
that September day, the rifles, shotguns,
poking out above the walls, waiting.
I think of the Convent of the Capuchins
in Rome,
where the monks led us
into their cavern of 4000 skulls,
intricate figures re-shaped from the fallen,
a grinning dance of death.

Portrait of my father
with Caravaggio's hands

He starts a charcoal sketch,
a quick one of Island Lake—
the summer mist lifts.
Now he fleshes out the background
and shifts to color.
I see him turn toward me—
I'm better with faces and people
than landscape.

And instead of Dante's head
or a bust of Raphael,
he gets the whole of it—
a crowded gallery of faces.
His hands are not curled or shaking,
but thick, articulate,
able to get the eyes right, the brow.
He looks at his hands
and thinks of Caravaggio,
of the silver coast—
the boats at anchor there.

I see my father swim into deep water,
doing the crawl—
he moves in graceful strokes toward a raft
anchored in the waves.
I see his arms rise and fall
in the dark blue water.
I call out to him
as if it were still summer,
and a son could call his father back
from the edge of that world.

Cinque

you'll go down if you don't stand up for yourself—
surely you see that...
—Brecht

All the way to the Lido and back
the stops churned past
and we were warmed by the rain.
You said let's pretend
we're Italians
and when the tourists
come aboard, let's keep saying *cinque*.
But that night the vaporetto
took us too far,
and as the boat careened in the new storm
we were thrown together you and I,
your hands held my hands,
our fingers intertwined.
Like another night
when locked in a coaster car,
poised atop thin metal rails
we stared over the edge
agape, straining to let go.

To know this fear, this wave
that reaches up to carry us away
is to know the other side—
the bottomless, tumbling slide
wild shouts and the wave of hair.
This plunge from shadow to shadow,
this chance, a few moments
out in the open.

for Nicholas

Nanticoke

What were we looking for
that winter morning
Carl and I drove the interstate West
across Northern Pennsylvania,
the road leading past Webster's Crossing,
Varysburg, and Doc's Garage
where they towed the highway wrecks.

Did we believe we'd get away?
Past the packing plants, the tanneries,
the open factory lots.
Past the worker bars—Butchko's, Dominic's,
The Hilltop.
Past the empty playing fields,
the stone bleachers edged with snow.
Until farther up, above St. Anthony's
only pine woods, open fields.

Is it enough to move
and not look back?

*

The fall night Shaw drove his '63 Corvette
into a tree in Groveland Station,
we were dancing at the Lakeshore.
Sam Cappy brought us the news the next day,
and we stood apart, drinking coffee.

You thought of Shaw's quick good looks,
the way he stared as if he were
somewhere else.
I don't know, he said,

right when you think you've got some time,
it all goes flat.

*

One day in late spring
on the road to Radicofani,
I stopped the car to pick some roadside flowers,
poppies and blue mountain laurel —
we heard the bells
before we saw the sheep clustered on the hillside.

Later, we looked down from the tower,
and the boys thought the world
was moving away from us.

Is it the light
that calls us from silence?

*

In my dream a voice says:
you have to get to the end of something
to get a sense of how it started.

There is a rusted iron bridge
buttressed by stone,
a creek widening beneath the trestle,
choked with branches, snarls of fishing line,
broken glass.
The sharp cries of a jay in the hop hornbeam,
and your hand lifting me up into this present.

Grappa in November
for my brother, Dennis

The first thing I forgot was your voice.
I forgot the face in the window was your face.

Then I forgot the rain streaking the glass.
I forgot your cries.

I forgot the afternoons you waited for anyone,
for another voice to find you there, locked in—alone.

I forgot the bells, the leaves fell
the frost rimmed the edge of fields.

I forgot the fields.
I forgot the pine trees and the scent of pines.

I forgot the electric light under the bare trees,
the childhood spent in dreams.

I forgot what it was like to climb up
in the branches, refusing to come down.

*

There is the morning we awoke to a herd of horses
who grazed on rosemary bushes in the open yard,

eight or ten of them, broken loose from the stable
below the hill, snorting and nudging one another in the damp grass.

A man turns from the dust of the pale green path,
behind him, the vines stretch like a tier of sagging stairs.

Near the wooden gate, he pauses
to look back, his white shirtsleeves rolled up.

He sings a song to himself. His voice alone brings back
the farmhouse, the table set out in the open.

Wildflowers pressed in the pages
of a book, the dust of pollen on the fingers.

American Cemetery at Nettuno

Pope Clement VI guarded himself from plague
by sitting all summer between two fires.
The heat killed off the fleas
and burnt the ceiling black.
He lived to see the corpses piled up, the ceiling
painted over.
The knack for knowing how to cope
lies in how to know what comes back.
These crosses seem to sway and curve —
their lines extend away, their names
are all the places that were them.
No fires kept these fallen from harm's way.
The day's too hot, the breeze is stifling
calm and hot. My sons say,
Dad the ocean's there behind us,
you can hear the waves.
But all I hear are cars,
the tires rush against the road.
The gateman lets us in. *Bevelaqua,*
he says. His name means drink of water.
The day's on fire.
These dead come back—almost a fourth of all
who lie here—named or unnamed
are Italian.
They sent the homeboys back
to fight in Sicily and Anzio.
The dusk is coming on,
there are too many names.

Sorrow comes throwing stones

This morning
a mockingbird in the box leaf maple
sings a cardinal's song.
It's early, first light,
and I think of my father
almost a year
and still I see him, or feel his presence—
he holds a coffee cup with both hands
like he used to do,
or whistles to himself
in that thin repetitive kind of humming.
And for a few minutes I hear
the Johnny Hartman song he loved,
and I see him
dancing with my wife.
He shuffles backward in that way he had,
graceful, he sings the refrain—
You are too beautiful.
That quick riff and the mockingbird's
bad rendition of the cardinal
make me realize my father is really gone.
You think you know how you'll feel,
but grief is a surprise, it comes close
like a hand on your shoulder
and you look up,
afraid to admit your fear.

The last one left

The door is still open
and beyond the door, a room—
don't confuse it with any other.
All day the world enters and leaves,
the night is full of what the day has left:
small sounds, breezes, the smell of salt,
and what else?
A pomegranate, an orange,
a taste that memory enhances.
The way the wind lifts the curtains,
outside the smell of leaves—
a green that comes back, even now.
The rest, all those other greens
have run away.
Only numbers keep adding up,
little sparrow nesting in the tulip poplar
stay awhile.
A song this morning
and the rain later,
the sound of the rain on the wet road.

Spanish Steps

Maybe you can get away,
maybe the whole long story
has a place after all—*sure* Greco says,
like the two young women who threw
drinks in your face
the night you told them
a little truth, they wanted to get back
somehow, the way talk
goes from bad to worse.

And now it's just these friends
who've led you back
through crowds,
the march for *pace*
over, the streets closed off.
You walked all the way
to find the little chapel of San Silvestro
where nuns sang a cappella the chants
of peace, the tiny wooden door
opening to take the change—and later
the church of the Quattro Coronati,
and then the piazza,
the streets leading down again.
Those songs stay with you still,
hymns to a stillness, unheard
and sweet.

Oh, how many years
since a boy stood on the edge of the dark
and asked you to come back?
Howard Camp, where the crop was almost in,
the season ended,
the workers on the move again.
How many times have you gone back
to stand alone in that growing dark

and ask the same things, waiting for the truck
to come. The crew boss angry
that you'd stayed too late.
You still see his hands.

Pilgrims, your Italian friends say,
pilgrims who've come to see the barque,
Bernini's fountain beneath the rooms
where Keats and Severn stayed.
I lost my son here once you tell them,
he ran ahead of us, down into the crowds at night.
He was six years old then, panic hit.
And there below, at last
we saw him—
playing chess with older Roman boys
who'd gathered to watch him play.
It's like that really, the quick
sting of loss that comes
because you're honest and don't know how
to cover up. A death so sharp and quick
it takes your breath away, an infant son's death,
his hands so small they cling to your finger
holding on for life. You cannot
turn away.

We took our sons to Cumae,
to see the cave where Aeneas
asked the Sybil for advice,
we saw the sea beyond
the caves, and climbed the stairs.
How sad Montale said
*memory at its fullest
has no one to hold it back.*
And still this small hand reaches out
like foreign voices chanting songs of peace,
a view from shuttered rooms along a river,
silver coins tossed into a moving stream.

Notes

Lines from Paul Zweig are from *Eternity's Woods*, Wesleyan University Press, 1985.

"On a line from Li Po"—based on a translation from the Chinese by David Hinton.

"Gathering firewood at Chimney Mountain"—lines in italics are from Pierre Reverdy.

"Don't look back" from the Temptations' song—lyrics by W. Robinson & R. White. Lines from Raymond Patterson from his poem "I've Got a Home in that Rock."

"Hook Mountain Lookout"—lines from Harry Beacon (aka Harry Nelson) are from *Inside: Writings by Attica Inmates—1977*.

"A small song for Luke" is for my son, Luke 2/17/02-2/29/02.

"*Ora e sempre*"—"now and always or now and forever." Constantine Brumidi—fresco painter of the Capitol in Washington, D.C.

"Jumper"—lines from Guido Gozzano are translated by Michael Palma.

"Attica 1977"—opening line is from a poem by Dave Kelly. Title taken from a poem by Sharif Lateef aka Ray Chunn.

"*Cinque*"—"wild shouts and the wave of hair" is from Stephen Crane's "The Black Riders."

"Grappa in November"—title is adapted from Cesare Pavese's "Grappa in September" in *Lavorare Stanca*. The line "the first thing I forgot. . ." is from Pedro Salinas.

"*Mi ricordo*" and "The last one left"—lines in italics are loosely borrowed from Cesar Vallejo's *Trilce*.

"Spanish Steps"—over three million people participated in the peace march in Rome in February 2003 against the U.S. invasion of Iraq.

About the Author

Gerald McCarthy was born in Endicott, New York, the eldest son of an Italian mother and Irish–American father. He left home at age seventeen to join the Marines, served a tour of duty in Vietnam, then deserted the military. After he was released from military prison and civilian jail, McCarthy worked as a stonecutter, shoe factory worker and anti-war activist. Later he attended the University of Iowa's Writers Workshop and taught writing at Attica Prison and in migrant labor camps, jails and schools. McCarthy has published two volumes of poetry, *War Story* (1977) and a chapbook, *Shoetown* (1992). He has lived and traveled widely in Italy. He teaches writing at St. Thomas Aquinas College and lives with his wife Michele and their sons Nicholas, Ben and Nate in Nyack, New York.